$16.85
GARRETT 01

W9-CBE-200

RACE CAR LEGENDS

The Allisons
Mario Andretti
Crashes & Collisions
Demolition Derby
Drag Racing
Dale Earnhardt
Famous Finishes
Formula One Racing
A. J. Foyt
Jeff Gordon
The History of NASCAR
Kenny Irwin
The Jarretts
The Labonte Brothers
The Making of a Race Car
Mark Martin
Jeremy Mayfield
Monster Trucks & Tractors
Motorcycles
Richard Petty
The Pit Crew
Stunt Driving
The Unsers
Rusty Wallace
Women in Racing

CHELSEA HOUSE PUBLISHERS

RACE CAR LEGENDS

THE ALLISONS
America's First Family of Stock-car Racing

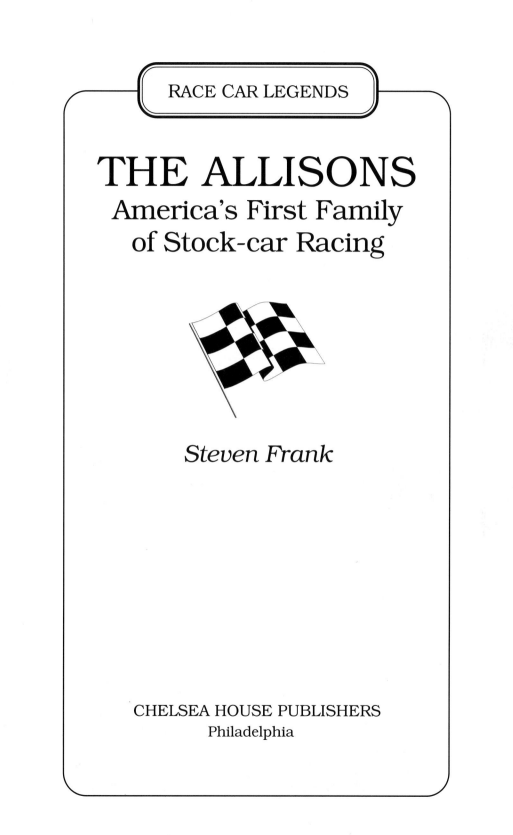

Steven Frank

CHELSEA HOUSE PUBLISHERS
Philadelphia

Produced by Daniel Bial and Associates
New York, New York

Picture research by Alan Gottlieb
Cover illustration by Neil Maclachlan

Frontispiece photo: Bobby Allison

The Chelsea House World Wide Website address is
http://www.chelseahouse.com

5 7 9 8 6 4

Library of Congress Cataloging-in-Publication Data

Frank, Steven
     The Allisons / Steven Frank.
        p.   cm. — (Race car legends)
     Includes bibliographical references and index.
     Summary   A biography which focuses on the racing careers of Bobby
and Davey Allison, the father and son automobile racing champions.
     ISBN 0-7910-3184-5. — ISBN 0-7910-3185-3 (pbk.)
     1. Allison, Bobby. —Juvenile literature. 2. Allison, Davey. 1961– or 2–
—Juvenile literature. 3. Automobile racing drivers—United States—Biography—Juvenile literature.
     [1. Allison, Bobby. 2. Allison, Davey. 1961– or 2– 3. Automobile
racing drivers.]
I. Title. II. Series
GV1032.A3F73   1996
796.7′2′092 B—dc20
                                      95-18673
                                         CIP
                                         AC

Acknowledgments

I would like to thank Paul Taublieb, executive in charge of production
of *The Davey Allison Story,* for providing me with a copy of his tape.

CONTENTS

INTRODUCTION   6

CHAPTER 1
IT RUNS IN THE FAMILY   9

CHAPTER 2
THE ALLISON BROTHERS
HIT THE ROAD   17

CHAPTER 3
SPEEDING TO SUCCESS   23

CHAPTER 4
BOBBY IN VICTORY LANE   33

CHAPTER 5
LIKE FATHER, LIKE SON   43

CHAPTER 6
LIFE IN THE FAST LANE   53

STATISTICS   61
CHRONOLOGY   62
FURTHER READING   63
INDEX   64

THE DRIVE TO WIN

What's the most popular spectator sport in the United States? It's not baseball, football, basketball, or even horse racing. America's favorite sport is automobile racing.

To the outsider, it looks simple. You get in your car, keep the accelerator depressed as you hurtle around the track, expect your crew to keep the car in perfect condition, and try not to go deaf as you weave your machine through traffic toward the checkered flag. But in actuality, it's not at all easy. Just as baseball isn't simply a matter of hitting the ball, so racing is full of subtleties.

What does it take to be a world-class race car driver? The more you know about the lives of the greats, the more it becomes clear that each successful driver is an extraordinary athlete gifted with unusual vision, coordination, and the will to win. The concentration necessary to send a car speeding around a track at 200 miles per hour for hour after hour, when a momentary lapse can cause instant death for him and any unfortunate driver near him, is phenomenal. Any driver worth his salt must be strong, self-confident, resilient, and willing to take risks in order to have an opportunity to win.

In addition, the top drivers have to be good businessmen and know how to put together a winning team. They have to find sponsors to put them in competitive cars. They rely on a pit crew to make sure that their car is always in peak performance condition. And they have to be mentally prepared each race day to take into consideration a host of factors: weather, the other racers, the condition of the track, and how their car is responding on that day. Without everything right, a driver won't stand a chance of winning.

All the drivers in the Race Car Legends series grew up around race cars. The fathers of Richard Petty and Dale Earnhardt were very successful race car drivers themselves. A. J. Foyt's father was a part-time racer and a full-time mechanic; the Allisons and Unsers are an extended family of racers. Only Mario Andretti's father disapproved of his son's racing. Yet Mario and his twin brother Aldo devoted themselves to racing at a young age.

Despite the knowledge and connections a family can provide, few of the legendary racers portrayed in this series met with immediate success. They needed to prove themselves in sprint cars or midget cars before they were allowed to get behind the wheel of a contending stock car or a phenomenally expensive Indy car. They needed to be tested in the tough races on the hardscrabble tracks before they learned enough to handle the race situations at Daytona or the Brickyard. They needed to learn how to get the most out of whatever vehicle they were piloting, including knowing how to fix an engine in the wee hours of the night before a big race.

A driver also has to learn to face adversity, because crashes often take the lives of friends or relatives. Indeed, every driver has been lucky at one point or another to survive a scare or a bad accident. "We've had our tragedies, but what family hasn't?" remarked the mother of Al and Bobby Unser. "I don't blame racing. I love racing as our whole family has."

What each driver has proved is that success in this most grueling sport takes commitment. Walter Payton, the great football running back, and Paul Newman, star of many blockbuster movies, have both taken up racing—and proved they have some talent behind the wheel. Still, it's evident that neither has been able to provide the devotion it takes to be successful at the highest levels.

To be a great driver, racing has to be in your blood.

1

IT RUNS IN THE FAMILY

Before the start of the 1988 Daytona 500, Bobby Allison was asked what he planned to do if he found himself in the lead during the final lap of the 200-lap auto race. "Hold it down and keep going," Bobby replied, "and dare the other guy to make a try at you." He didn't realize that when it came down to the final laps, the other guy he found himself up against would be his own son, Davey.

Both on and off the track, the Allisons were familiar faces in the world of stock-car racing. The Allison name had first become known in racing circles over 25 years before, when Bobby and his brother Donnie began racing at the smaller short tracks of the Southeast.

Bobby and Donnie soon began racing at the larger, faster superspeedways, always bringing the family along with them to cheer them on. Their parents, E. J. and Kittie Allison, were such familiar faces at the track that other racers called

Bobby Allison's number 12 car on the way to victory at the 1988 Daytona 500

them "Mom" and "Pop." Together, the family became known as the "Alabama Gang." At the 1988 Daytona 500, the world had a chance to see this racing family at its best.

Stock-car races are primarily run by the National Association for Stock Car Auto Racing (NASCAR). The most important series of races run by NASCAR are the Winston Cup Grand Nationals. The Grand Nationals are the major leagues of racing, featuring only the most experienced and talented drivers.

The first race of the Winston Cup season is the Daytona 500. The 200-lap, 500-hundred mile race is the ultimate test of speed, skill, and endurance. Every February, about 150,000 spectators crowd the stands at Daytona International Speedway in Daytona Beach, Florida, to watch this important race. Millions more watch on television.

At the 1988 Daytona 500, Bobby Allison came into the race an old pro; at 50 years old, he'd already won the Daytona twice. In 1988, he was the only one of the top 14 drivers in the race to have previously won the Daytona. On the other hand, it was only the second time 26-year-old Davey was competing at Daytona.

Nevertheless, Davey had already created a stir in the racing world. In 1987, he had been named NASCAR rookie of the year. He had also set a record at that year's Daytona. Davey became the first rookie ever to start the Daytona 500 from the first row.

In 1988, Davey once again qualified for a place in the front row, a few rows in front of his father. When the flagman waved the green flag signaling the start of the race, Davey and Bobby led the pack of cars down the front straightaway.

The two Allisons, father and son, were soon racing side by side.

During the previous season, Bobby was involved in a major accident at the super speedway in Talladega, Alabama. Bobby was going about 210 mph when his car slid alongside the fence, forcing it into the air like an out-of-control pinwheel. Fortunately, no one was seriously injured. However, as a result of that incident, NASCAR decided to take measures to reduce the risk at the races by cutting down the cars' speeds. They ordered all drivers to attach a plate to the vehicles that chokes off the air supply to the engine and reduces the horsepower. Rather than a speed of around 210 mph, drivers would now have a maximum rate of about 193 mph.

Fortunately, the speed reduction didn't make for a less exciting race. For one thing, 193 mph

Although the Allisons have a close family, on the race track things were different. At the 1979 Daytona 500, Donnie Allison (in the number 1 car) gets hit by brother Bobby (number 15). Neither was seriously injured.

is still plenty fast (think of it as being more than three times as fast as you'd ever go in your own car on the freeway). Moreover, changes made to the cars' spoiler—the plate mounted to the car's rear deck to keep it stable at high speeds—made the cars much more difficult to control.

That the Daytona track was as fast and furious as ever became clear to everyone about halfway through the 1988 race. Richard Petty, considered the king of stock-car racing due to his record of 200 NASCAR wins (including seven Daytona 500s), was involved in a heart-stopping crash. As he came out of a turn in lap 106, Petty's car began to skid. Another car coming around the turn smashed into Petty and sent his car into the wall, where the impact forced the vehicle to rise straight into the air. After gracefully diving back down to earth headfirst, Petty flipped six times, all the while shedding bits of sheet metal and scraps of tire.

When Brett Bodine tried to move past Petty's car, he ran over a piece of sharp metal that sliced his rear tire. The air quickly escaped from the tire and Bodine's car began to skid and careened into Petty's. The force of the impact sent Petty once again spinning into the cement wall, where he finally came to an abrupt stop.

Miraculously, Petty came out of this massive crash without a serious injury. He was even able to walk out of the hospital a few hours later. For the other drivers still in the race, though, the crash meant 21 laps racing under a yellow caution flag while the crew made repairs to the track. The yellow caution flag flies after any type of accident and means the drivers must slow down until the track is cleared. No passing is allowed. When the green flag is once again displayed, drivers can return to normal speeds and strategies.

When Bobby saw the green flag, he took it as an opportunity to push for the lead. While other cars struggled to work up more speed, Bobby gunned his engine and quickly thrust to the front. Davey, not far behind, quickly followed, not wanting to let his father get a big lead.

For the Allisons, the new speed restrictions ironically proved to work to their advantage. As a result of the cars' slower speeds, most drivers relied on a technique known as "cooperative drafting" to work up speed. When cars race at high speeds they meet resistance from the air in front of them, which slows them down. Cars line up directly behind the lead car so they won't face the same resistance; the lead car pushes through the wall of air and leaves a nice clear pocket of air. If a car pulls into that pocket, it gets pulled along with the lead car. The second car is then able to increase its speed without using as much energy; the lead car also benefits as it cuts through the air. During a race, you might see as many as 10 to 12 cars lined up, nose to tailpipe, to take advantage of the draft.

Naturally, the drawback to drafting is that as long as you're in the line of cars, you're not moving up in the standings. Thus drivers have to figure out when to break out of the line in order to pull ahead of the other cars, a technique known as "slingshotting."

It takes a really strong, well-built car to be able to do this successfully. That's what Buddy Baker discovered when he suddenly shot out of the line of cars coasting in the draft and tried to pick up enough speed to pass Bobby Allison in front. Once outside the draft, the air hit Baker's car like a brick wall, slowing him down and leaving him far behind the pack of cars.

At the 1988 Daytona, Bobby clearly had the superior car. When drivers lined up behind him to take advantage of the draft, most were unable to work up enough speed to slingshot past him.

After winning the 1988 Daytona 500, Bobby holds the trophy—and is dowsed with soda.

Throughout the race, while cars were falling apart and falling behind, Bobby's Buick Regal remained comfortably in the lead.

During the final laps of the race, there were 17 drivers who were on the same lap—the most in the history of the Daytona— and Bobby was at the head of the pack.

With only about 10 laps to go, Bobby looked behind him and saw one other competitor who had a car strong enough to make the pass: his own son Davey.

The night before the race, Davey's Ford Thunderbird had crashed during a practice round. But Davey had spent many years working in his father's garage, and he had learned how to make his own repairs. He spent the entire night rebuilding his car. By the start of the race, his vehicle was once again in top shape. He alone was able to keep up with Bobby in the final laps—and he gave his father the race of his life.

When asked later on if he considered just letting his father win, Davey said, "Never." In his mind, it wasn't his father who was two car lengths ahead of him—it was his opponent. And Davey wanted to take home that trophy himself.

Davey slingshotted out of the draft and closed the distance Bobby had tried to put between them. As the two cars raced toward the finish line, they were virtually side by side. Bobby and Davey were close enough to see each other behind the wheel.

Davey had his car running full out, but his father's positioning had been too good. Davey's Thunderbird just could not match the momentum his father's Buick had built. When the checkered flag was waved to signal the end of the race, it was Bobby who had crossed the finish line first. Davey came in only a few seconds later.

With that win, Bobby's third Daytona victory, he became the only 50-year-old driver to win the race as well as the oldest man to win a Winston Cup race. Davey would go on to his own moments of racing glory, including winning the Daytona in 1992. When asked which race was his favorite, Davey responded that it was not one of his many victories that meant the most to him; it was the race in which he came in second place. Because that was the race he had the honor of losing to the great Bobby Allison—his father.

2

THE ALLISON BROTHERS HIT THE ROAD

In 1959, 21-year-old Bobby Allison and his younger brother Donnie, aged 19, hopped in a pickup truck and took to the open road. They weren't exactly certain where they were going, but at long last they were doing what they loved. They were racing cars.

The sons of a service station equipment supplier, they had grown up in Miami, Florida, in a large family that numbered 13 brothers and sisters. From the time Bobby and Donnie were young they loved to go to the racetrack, experiencing the thrills and excitement of the sport.

When Bobby was nine years old, his grandfather took him to a local track to see his first race. Sitting in the stands, watching the cars zoom around the track while the crowd cheered, Bobby decided he wanted to become a race car driver.

Of course, he had several years to go before he would even be old enough to drive, much less

In the late 1950s, the Allison brothers wanted to leave Miami in order to start their racing career.

compete in a race. Bobby couldn't wait to get behind the wheel of a car. On his 14th birthday, he rushed out and got his Florida driver's license.

When he started high school, he had saved up enough money to buy his own car. Since this was his first car, it held a special place in his heart. He spent hours and hours taking care of it. He drove it to school every day. On the way home, he usually stopped at an empty field where he would race in circles, pushing the car to go faster and faster until he could get it to spin out.

When Bobby was a senior, he talked his parents into letting him drive in a race at a local Florida track, the Hialeah Speedway. Against 54 other racers, he finished 10th, a very respectable performance. His confidence boosted by this debut, Bobbie continued to compete at local tracks. For the most part, these races were not noteworthy. Bobby did, however, break some records at Hialeah—not for setting high speeds, but for rolling his car over. He was the first amateur at Hialeah to roll a car and soon became the first one to roll a car *twice*.

As you might imagine, his parents were not so pleased with this record. Fearing for their son's safety, they forbade Bobby from ever racing again.

After his high school graduation, Bobby put his love of cars into mechanics rather than racing. He got a job testing outboard motorboat engines for a company called Mercury Outboard located in Wisconsin. For a while, the job fulfilled Bobby's craving for action; to test the motors, he had to race boats across the water at top speeds. But boats weren't cars, and Bobby still dreamed of a career in stock-car racing.

In 1956, he moved back to Miami, now with enough knowledge of motors to open his own garage. While working as a mechanic, Bobby gained an intimate understanding of what makes cars run and, more importantly, what to do to make them run faster. He soon put this knowledge to work and built his own souped-up racing car from a 1934 Chevy coupe.

Once again, Bobby began racing at the local Florida racetracks. But he now had to do it in secret. He didn't want his parents to know he was racing, so he drove under an alias. When Bobby's parents read in the newspaper about a driver named Robert Sunderman, they had no idea it was their own son Bobby.

This went on for some time until, one night at dinner, Bobby's brother Tommy accidentally let the cat out of the bag and told their parents about Bobby's secret identity. By then, Bobby was well on his way to a successful racing career. In the Chevy, Bobby had won races all over the Miami area. His parents saw how dedicated Bobby was to the sport and eventually supported his efforts.

Two freak accidents in 1958 changed Bobby's life. In September, he crashed at the Hollywood track and his car caught fire. Watching from the stands was an attractive blonde woman named

In 1962, Bobby was back at West Palm Beach, racing his modified.

Judy, who became quite upset when she saw the accident. Her companion, who was a friend of Bobby's, decided she should at least meet the driver for whom she was so concerned. After the race, he introduced Judy to Bobby. A year later, Judy and Bobby were married.

The second major incident occurred when Bobby was at work in his garage and accidentally dropped a heavy automatic transmission on his hand. Although the injury kept Bobby from racing for several weeks, it made him realize something important. He realized that if he was going to get hurt, it might as well be doing something he enjoyed. From that day on, Bobby committed himself to a serious racing career.

Meanwhile, Bobby's younger brother Donnie also started racing. Unlike Bobby, auto racing was not Donnie's first true love. Donnie loved horse racing and dreamed of being a jockey. His hopes were ruined after a serious motorcycle accident landed him in the hospital for four months. While recuperating, he gained 30 pounds, making him much too heavy to be a jockey.

He could, though, still be a stock-car driver. He began to accompany Bobby to races at the local tracks. One night at Hialeah, he heckled the driver of a 1941 Ford for his slow showing. The driver of the Ford dared Donnie to do better. Donnie did, pushing the car on to faster speeds than the first man ever had. Donnie repeated this amazing feat the following week as well. The driver—who also owned the car—was so impressed he turned the car over to Donnie.

While Bobby was making a name for himself in the main events, known as the "feature" races, Donnie was driving regularly in the smaller amateur races. One night, friends talked Bobby into letting Donnie drive in a feature race. Bobby reluctantly agreed, only to see his brother crash into a fence and destroy the car.

Once Bobby had seen that Donnie was not seriously injured, he yelled at his brother and insulted Donnie's driving. For Donnie, Bobby's words were a challenge. He set out to prove himself as a serious race car driver.

In 1959, the brothers decided to leave Miami to get experience on other racetracks. With no particular destination in mind, they headed toward Alabama looking for better opportunities to race. The two traveled from town to town, sleeping in the back of a pickup truck, racing at the smaller tracks they came across.

Eventually, they settled down in Hueytown, Alabama, mostly because it was close to the modified racing circuit of the Southeast. This large racing circuit, stretching from northern Louisiana through the Carolinas to Virginia, encompasses many tracks that provided plenty of chances for the brothers to race. Bobby and Donnie were able to compete almost every night of the week.

In Alabama, Bobby eventually settled into a modest brick house, where he and Judy raised their four children, Davey, Bonnie, Carrie, and Clifford. He moved his parents to a mobile home right across the street. Donnie and his wife, Pat, settled nearby with their children, Pam, Kenney, Ronald, and Donald. Fortunately, Bobby's house had a nice living room where all these family members could come by for a visit.

In no time, that living room also became filled with trophies.

3
SPEEDING TO SUCCESS

During the 1960s, Bobby and Donnie competed primarily in the modified division. These races are known as the testing grounds for young drivers hoping to make it into NASCAR's major league, the Grand Nationals.

The cars in these races, unlike the slick, professionally built newer models in the Grand Nationals, are older models that the drivers soup up themselves. Bobby and Donnie virtually had to rebuild their cars after each race. Sometimes, they could barely afford to pay for the parts they needed. Bobby once showed up at a race in Richmond, Virginia, without enough money to pay for tires and was forced to borrow a set from another driver.

Bobby and Donnie raced three, four, or even five nights a week, hoping to win enough money to be able to race again the following week. They often had to drive all night and all day to make

Bobby Allison, after setting the lap record of 197.573 mph at the Alabama International Raceway at Taladega, in 1969.

it to the next race on time—and then they had to hop into the race car and do their best with only a couple of hours of sleep.

The modified circuit is known to be extremely rough. The drivers are very tough and fiercely competitive both on and off the track. The local drivers gang up on drivers from out of town and try to knock them out of the race. Bobby and Donnie often found themselves having to fend off these attacks on the track.

There are many unwritten rules in racing, especially for rookies. These rules dictate such things as who you can hit and how hard, who you can block, and who you must always allow to pass you by. Early on, Bobby earned a reputation for breaking those rules. Bobby brushed against other cars and tried to force them into the wall or onto the grassy infield. He even did this with the older, more experienced drivers, which was a real taboo. However, Bobby impressed everyone by his refusal to back down from a confrontation. People saw that Bobby had the kind of guts and self-confidence needed to make it in the big time.

Once, at Huntsville, Alabama, four drivers teamed up to try to force Bobby out of the race. For the entire race, they surrounded Bobby's car and kept knocking into him from all sides. When Bobby tried to pass other cars to move ahead, these drivers blocked his path.

Between heats, he spoke to these drivers and asked them to lay off of him and give him room to pass them on the track. They played dumb and denied trying to block him. When the next part of the race started, though, they continued bumping him.

By the feature race of the day, three of the four drivers who were ganging up on Bobby remained. Bobby decided it was time for him to take action. He quickly knocked the first driver out of the race. Then, he bumped the second car hard enough to send it spinning in circles onto the infield. Finally, he pulled alongside the third car and quickly spun his steering wheel to the right, sending the other car into the wall. NASCAR officials condemned Bobby for this action and gave him a fine. But Bobby didn't have any more trouble from those drivers for the rest of the day.

In the early 1960s, Bobby drove in as many as 100 races a year on tracks all over the country. This experience gave him a tremendous advantage over other drivers. "When I would go to a city, I ran against drivers who were pretty good in their area, but, with all that traveling, there wasn't a track anywhere I wasn't familiar with. It had to give me an edge."

Donnie Allison poses with a checkered flag in anticipation of winning his next race.

During all those years when Bobby was racing on the modified circuit, he saw just about every kind of situation that could develop in a race. He also saw the different ways drivers handled these incidents and, most important, learned what strategies worked and what didn't. When he was in a race and a problem came up, Bobby was able to make split-second decisions about what to do.

Also, since Bobby made all his own repairs, he developed a keen understanding of how cars operate. This enabled him to develop ways to alter the car and improve its performance. It also helped when he was driving in a race. If the car wasn't running properly, Bobby knew how to use his driving to make up for the problem.

By 1965, Bobby had clearly mastered the modified circuit; he had twice won the NASCAR subcategory of the modified special championship, and had twice won the modified championship itself. When an elderly car owner named Betty Lilly offered him an opportunity to drive her Ford, he made the decision, at last, to move up to the Grand Nationals.

Most professional racing cars are owned by people other than the driver. The owners are responsible for the costs of maintaining the car and for paying the crew team and driver. Everybody splits the winnings. Many cars also have a corporate sponsor who contributes to the cost of the car. Usually, only experienced drivers with a proven track record are able to find a sponsor.

Bobby Allison (number 24) spins out of the way to avoid hitting Clyde Prickett. Prickett had just hit the bank at the 1966 Motor Trend 500, and seconds later Allison hit the bank, too. Neither was injured, although both cars were wrinkled.

Bobby raced for Mrs. Lilly for several months. But when the two had a disagreement regarding financial arrangements, Bobby decided to go into business for himself. He bought his own 1964 Chevelle and put his mechanical expertise to work. With about $6,000—a relatively small sum—and the help of his brothers Eddie and Donnie, he transformed the Chevelle into a 164-mph Grand National racing machine.

As an independent driver, Bobby had to make all his own repairs after every crash or fender bender. After each race, Bobby worked away at his own car day and night to make certain it was in top condition for the next race.

As an independent driver, Allison's first season in the Grand Nationals did have its setbacks, but it also had some spectacular highlights. Looking back on that first professional season, Bobby remembered it as having "the greatest joy and the greatest heartbreak, the greatest success and the greatest failure of any."

Bobby felt a tremendous thrill when he won his first two Grand National races at Oxford, Maine, and Islip, New York. But he also suffered an unfortunate loss at Martinsville, Virginia, when he managed to pass several cars within 23 laps to take the lead, only to lose in the final laps when his engine blew.

Racing in the Grand Nationals, Bobby almost immediately started attracting attention. Just as he had turned heads by breaking unwritten rules in the modified circuit, his first few seasons in the Grand Nationals found him making an impression for his aggressive, almost ruthless driving style.

In 1966, Bobby competed in the Winston-Salem, a short, 100-mile race around a half-mile dirt track. Although not an important race, it is extremely popular among the NASCAR drivers. Bobby, still a rookie in the Grand Nationals, shocked the racing world by bumping the car of Curtis Turner, an experienced professional who at the time had won the most stock-car races in history. Throughout the race, Allison and Turner continued knocking against one another, forcing one another to spin out of control, and slam-

Bobby Allison works on his car after leading the qualification race for the 1968 Firecracker 400.

ming each other into the wall. Both cars became covered with dents and scratches. Eventually, they knocked each other out of the race.

Off the track, Bobby's warmth and charm made him one of the most popular racers in the circuit among both fans and fellow drivers. After each race, he always met with his many fans, whom he considered his friends, to listen to their praise and even their criticism. He frequently made personal appearances at charitable events, such as for the Boy Scouts or for handicapped children. Several times, he was voted most popular Grand National driver in a NASCAR poll (he'd won it four times by 1982).

He was also known as a family man, completely devoted to his wife and children. He acted as the head of the large Allison family, often giving advice and help to his family members. For fun, he liked nothing better than a day of fly fishing or a night of bowling.

On the track, however, Bobby was quite a different person. Drivers considered him to be an extremely tough adversary. His personal motto was "whatever it takes" because he did whatever he needed to do in order to win.

Bobby was part of one of the most famous feuds in racing history in the 1960s and early 70s with Richard Petty, considered the greatest of all stock-car racers. Petty won the Winston Cup championship seven times; he also won the Daytona 500 seven times—far more than any other driver.

In a biography of Petty called *King Richard*, Bobby described the rivalry: "[Petty] was established, the top guy, and I was just coming on. He seemed to take the attitude he shouldn't be challenged. But I go into every race with the intention of doing whatever it takes to win and so does he. And our talent is close enough so, if our cars are about equal, sometimes he'll win and sometimes I'll win. We got to leaning on each other for a while, but I still respect him and I think he respects me."

In 1967, Bobby had been a champ in the modified division but was only a rookie in the Grand National circuit, where Petty had earned the nickname King. Late in the season, at a race in North Carolina, there was a minor fender bending incident between the two drivers, and it was unclear which driver had caused the accident. The following summer, another incident in Islip led to a fistfight between the two crews.

Petty and Bobby each blamed the other for starting the feud, claiming they had only reacted to a move initiated by the other driver. Bobby said he felt Petty had purposely decided to hit him at Islip, giving him not just a small tap but a major "cah-LUNK." In *King Richard*, Bobby said, "after that, I didn't hesitate to cah-LUNK him when the opportunity arose. We got to looking for each other, if you know what I mean. It just went on and on."

For five years, at both short track and Grand National superspeedway races, they would bump against one another on the track. At times, their skirmishes became dangerous, leading to major pileups. Eventually, though, the two met in person and put an official end to the feud. Throughout their careers, they maintained respect for one another's driving abilities.

Another rivalry that heated up the tracks was between Bobby and Donnie. Donnie had also moved up to the Grand National circuit in 1966 and was making a name for himself. In 1967, he finished in the top ten in seven different races and was nominated rookie of the year. In 1968, he did even better, finishing in the top five in five different races.

While the brothers had often faced one another on short tracks, they now found themselves racing one another in major racing events. On several occasions, the race came down to a climactic Allison vs. Allison showdown.

One of these events was the National 500, at the Charlotte Speedway, in October 1969. During the first lap, Donnie quickly took the lead and held it for much of the race. Bobby, in a Daytona Charger, stayed close behind him. The only other driver to keep close was Buddy Baker, in a Dodge Daytona. With only five laps left in

Donnie Allison, behind the wheel of a 1969 Ford, takes the checkered flag of the 1969 Firecracker 400.

the race, Baker ran out of gas and dropped out of the race. That left Donnie and Bobby battling it out for the win in the final laps of the race.

Bobby's Charger managed to creep up on Donnie's Ford Talladega. Bobby pulled up alongside Donnie and tried to pass him. Donnie crossed the finish line seconds ahead of his brother.

The 1971 Winston 500 featured one of the great NASCAR finishes of all time and a classic Allison vs. Allison moment. Bobby and Donnie were both driving Mercuries, and they kept battling for the lead with Buddy Baker and Dave Marcis, who were both driving Dodges. By the last 70 miles of the 500-mile race, each of the four drivers had held the lead at some point.

With only eight laps to the end, Marcis's engine caught fire. That left Donnie in the lead, with Buddy Baker and brother Bobby right behind him. The race came down to the final lap, with the three almost side by side.

Coming out of the final turn of the final lap, Donnie pulled slightly ahead of the other two. He sailed into the home stretch and won by the length of one car.

Bobby went on to have a spectacular season, one of the best of his career. He earned seven NASCAR superspeedway victories. In one year he nearly doubled all his previous winnings. But that Allison vs. Allison finish at Talladega proved that Donnie was an excellent racer in his own right. The Alabama gang drivers were fast becoming legendary. Fans knew that whenever an Allison was on the track, there were certain to be sparks.

4

BOBBY IN VICTORY LANE

The top award in stock-car racing is the Winston Cup champion. In the 1980s, the NASCAR Grand Nationals was renamed the Winston Cup series. You don't win the Winston Cup by winning only a single race; it takes an entire season of expert driving. During each race in the Winston Cup season, drivers receive a number of points depending on their performance in individual races. The driver who finishes first gets the most points; the driver who finishes second gets fewer, and so on. At the end of the season, the driver with the most total points takes home the Winston Cup crown and a bonus prize of $1 million. Consistent excellence is needed to compete; grabbing the checkered flag in a few races isn't enough.

In the final race of the 1983 season, the Winston Western 500, Bobby only needed a decent finish to win the Winston Cup. He finished in ninth place—but that was still good enough to

Donnie Allison offers advice to Janet Guthrie, one of the few female drivers to compete in NASCAR races.

make him the champ. It was the top award Bobby won and the highlight of his career.

The win was a testimony to Bobby's incredible perseverance. It had taken over 20 years of racing to reach this moment. At times, Bobby had come awfully close to winning the crown; in 1981 and 1982, he came in second place, losing by only a handful of points. But Bobby didn't get discouraged by those close losses. Each year, he came back more determined than ever to do his best.

In the late 1970s, Bobby overcame the worst slump of his career, a dry period considered to be one of the worst in racing history. The trouble started in 1976, when Bobby was involved in two serious crashes only four months apart.

At the Carolina 500 in Rockingham, North Carolina, in February, a major collision landed him in the hospital for four days with a broken sternum, broken ribs, and serious internal bruises. The second accident took place at a short track in Elko, Minnesota, on a Saturday night in July. When Bobbie's car skidded in some oil, it went sailing into the concrete abutment. The impact left the car smashed beyond recognition. This time, Bobby had 11 broken bones, several in his face and feet, and required 40 stitches near his right eye, his cheek, and lip. Bobby remained in the hospital for five days.

Bobby refused to let these injuries foil his chance at a Winston Cup victory. A race was coming up that weekend, and Bobby wanted to earn the points. Although he had just returned home from the hospital, Bobby turned right around and headed to Nashville in a motor home with friend and fellow racer Neil Bonnett. Even with all his injuries, Bobby managed to qualify for the race and to run the first lap before Bonnett took over the wheel. According to the Winston Cup rules, since he had started the race Bobby was able to receive his points.

The following season was an all-time low for Bobby. He had no one offering to sponsor him, so he ran as an independent. Bobby found he lacked energy and was experiencing intense stomach pains. But he remained in the competition. "Even when I was sick real bad I could muster up my competitiveness. The one thing I could still do was get in that race car and drive," he said.

After the two accidents, Bobby raced in 67 races without a single win. In 1978, though, Bobby came back strong. Car owner Bud Moore knew of Bobby's abilities and past victories; despite Bobby's slump, he believed in Bobby as a driver and hired him to drive his car. As a result, the start of the season found Bobby driving Moore's enormous Thunderbird, which he nicknamed the "Luxury Liner."

Things didn't look so promising for Bobby during the qualifying race of that year's Daytona 500. Another car driven by Buddy Baker slid into him, leaving the Luxury Liner a wrecked hunk of metal.

While the crew was working on the car, Bobby went to a nearby camper to relax. After his depressing previous season, this qualifying race seemed like a pretty bleak omen. Bobby felt his hopes and his strength slipping away. When he came back to the shop, Allison saw that the crew had miraculously brought the car back to life. He couldn't even tell it had been in a crash. This really helped boost Bobby's confidence. Bobby thought to himself, "If these guys can do that for me, by God I'm going to drive that car the best I can."

Since he hadn't finished the qualifying race, Bobby had to start the Daytona in the 33rd position. Yet Bobby was now determined to do his best and refused to let the past season affect his confidence any longer.

For the first 60 laps, the race went smoothly. The drivers set record speeds and there were no caution flags. During these early laps, Bobby drove pretty steadily, just trying to keep up speed with the other cars.

In about the 68th lap of the race, Cale Yarborough was in the lead, with Benny Parsons behind him. Parsons suddenly blew a tire and started spinning out. In trying to avoid Parsons, Lennie Pond tapped A. J. Foyt, sending Foyt's Buick flipping head over tail. While trying to maneuver around Foyt, Bobby slid into Ron Hutcherson. The collision was not a serious one, though, and Bobby was able to continue.

The caution period following the crash enabled Bobby to move closer to the lead. In the 117th lap, however, he tried to pass Hutcherson and got squeezed against the wall. Both sides of the Thunderbird were banged up pretty badly, and the steering wheel was knocked out of kilter for the rest of the race. The impact also caused the front fender to bend into the tire. A lap later the tire blew, forcing Bobby to take a pit stop to change it.

With about 18 laps remaining, Bobby and Buddy Baker emerged as the two front-runners. For the rest of the race, they tried to outrun one another to take the lead. Neither had won the Daytona before and they were both hungry for victory.

With four laps remaining, Bobby got a lucky break. Baker's engine blew, forcing him out of the race. Now Bobby held the lead. And there wasn't anyone around who could mount a real challenge.

For years, Bobby had been a successful NASCAR driver, but the Daytona crown had always eluded him. Several times, Bobby lost the Daytona by only a few seconds. This time, though, Bobby crossed the finish line 33.2 seconds ahead of Cale Yarborough to take the race. After 18 years of trying, Bobby had at last won the Daytona 500. And what better race could you win to put an end to a 67-race losing streak?

Still recovering from his injuries and trying to regain his strength, Bobby won four more Winston Cup races in 1978 and finished second in the Winston Cup standings.

One of the reasons Bobby believes it took so long for him to take the Winston Cup was because he was always switching teams. In December 1981, however, Bobby signed on to a new team—DiGard/Gatorade. This new team made a big difference for Bobby, bringing him six wins in the 1982 season and a significant amount of Winston Cup points. The crew, led by Gary Nelson, admired Bobby as a driver and gave him a great deal of encouragement. Rather than arguing with one another, Bobby and his team worked well together and respected each other's ideas. With the stability of a top team behind him, Bobby was able to pay full attention to his driving.

Right from the start of the season, Bobby came on strong. As always, the first race of the season was the Daytona 500. The big day gave Bobby and his new team a real workout.

All these years that Bobby was racing in the Grand National circuit, he continued racing at short tracks and in the modified races as well. During the week, between Grand National races, his schedule would be filled with short track events. He even bought a plane so he could save time by flying from race to race.

The 1982 Daytona showed just how skillfully and intelligently Bobby could drive. After the fourth lap, Bobby made his move and pulled in front. But then, 10 miles into the race, Bobby was hit by Cale Yarborough from behind, sending the bumper of Bobby's car flying off onto the track. Five other cars knocked into the bumper and skidded off the track and out of the race.

Driving without a bumper seriously affected the way the car handled. But Bobby could use his extensive driving know-how to compensate for all the changes. Maintaining his speed, he was able to hold the lead.

As is typical in the Daytona 500, a long string of cars lined up behind one another to take advantage of the draft. Due to changes NASCAR made in the cars' designs that year, drivers were finding that they couldn't slingshot out of the line to pass the other cars. For most of the race, they remained in this head-tail formation.

For most of the race, Bobby was the one at the head of the line. He maintained the lead for 147 of the 200 laps.

About halfway through the race, another car blew its engine, sending shrapnel-like pieces of scrap metal and parts flying into the air and into Bobby's car. The burning engine also created a thick cloud of smoke.

As Bobby came around a turn, he drove directly into the smoke, leaving him unable to see

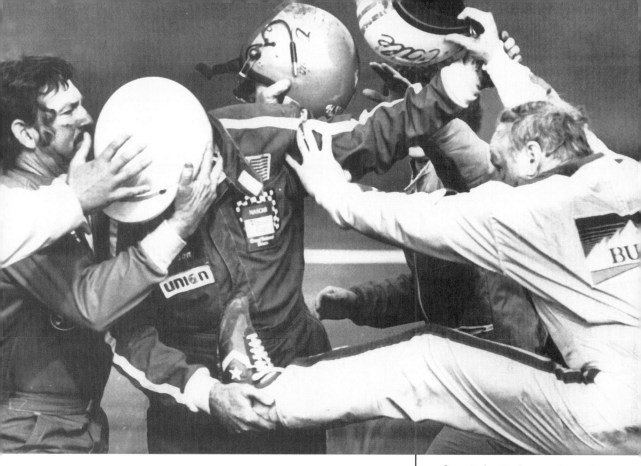

where he was going and what awaited him on the track ahead.

"I couldn't see nothing but smoke," Bobby later told *Sports Illustrated.* "I mean *nothing.* I couldn't see the racetrack, the other cars, the wall, *nothing.* I knew I was going to have to go in there blind. So I just backed off and squeezed up against the wall and held my breath."

Because he held back a bit, Bobby came out of the smoke unscathed. Other cars, however, were spinning all over the track, blindly smashing into one another.

Late in the race, Darrell Waltrip came up behind Bobby and tried to pass him to take the lead. Bobby had lost the Winston Cup crown to Waltrip last year. That loss made Bobby espe-

Bobby sits in his car, waiting out a 30-second penalty he incurred. He got the penalty for taking a short cut across the infield when he blew a tire at the 1982 Winston Western 500.

cially determined to beat out Waltrip in the current race.

After Waltrip passed him by, several other drivers also followed in the draft behind him. Bobby joined back in line, now in fifth place. Suddenly, Waltrip's engine blew, knocking him out of the race.

Bobby quickly took advantage of the situation. Under the cover of the cloud of smoke caused by Waltrip's blow, he pulled out of the draft and slingshotted ahead of the others. With about 50 miles left in the race, Bobby held the lead by about a mile. Finally, with only half a mile to go, Bobby's engine began to sputter. He was running out of gas. For a second, Bobby panicked, remembering last year's Daytona, when, only seconds from winning the race, he had run out of gas.

Bobby pushed the accelerator and prayed he would make it this year. He did run out of fuel. This time, fortunately, it was *after* he had crossed the finish line, taking his second Daytona win. Bobby was only the third driver, after Yarborough and Petty, to win the Daytona more than once.

Ironically, Bobby said his most satisfying race of that year was not the Daytona 500; it was a race he didn't even win.

The World 600 is the longest race on the NASCAR circuit and considered by many to be the most difficult. The conditions of the race are particularly grueling, as it takes place in Charlotte, North Carolina, in May, when the temperature reaches up into the 90s. Stock cars are not air-conditioned; the outside temperature, combined with the heat generated by the engine and the exhaust pipes, can raise the temperature inside the car well above 100 degrees. Drivers have been known to pass out upon exiting their vehicles.

Halfway through the race, the exhaust pipes on Bobby's Buick broke off, causing the floorboards of the car to heat to at least 1,000 degrees. The poisonous exhaust fumes blew into the car, making it difficult for Bobby to breathe. Bobby somehow managed to complete the race in these incredibly difficult circumstances.

This proved to Bobby that he had regained all his strength and was now once again one of the best in his sport. "I am the toughest," Bobby proudly told *Sports Illustrated*, "I am."

5

LIKE FATHER, LIKE SON

For Bobby's sons, Davey and Clifford, the racetrack was a second home. From the time they were little, they accompanied their parents to races, helping cheer on their father and uncle.

Across from the Allison family house in Hueytown was a wooded area in which the kids built their own bike track. Here, the Allison boys and other kids in the neighborhood held their own competitions. These races were modeled on the professional auto races they so often watched. They even used flags to signal the start and finish of the races.

At the bike races, when the kids chose which racer they wanted to pretend to be, Davey always chose Bobby. And he always won. His purple

Bobby Allison, coming off his Winston Cup championship, playfully adjusts the helmet of his 21-year-old son Davey before the 1981 West Grand Nationals, where Davey made his debut as a stock-car racer.

bicycle was a legend in the neighborhood.

When Davey was in school, he sometimes got himself into trouble because he spent the time he should have been doing classwork drawing pictures of the cars he dreamed of racing. As Davey got older, he realized it was time to stop dreaming about racing and start doing it. He worked for hours and hours in his father's shop, learning about how the cars ran and how to make repairs and improvements.

When he was older, Davey proudly spoke of all he had learned from his father, including some of Bobby's best driving tips. One of the main lessons he learned from Bobby was that he needed to make his own way in the racing world. Bobby's own father, "Pop" Allison, had taught him that if you earn something for yourself, you appreciate it even more. So Bobby knew it was important for Davey to work his way through the racing ranks on his own.

Just as his father had, Davey learned about racing by competing as often as possible. He got together with a few friends and formed his own team. As a joke, Bobby nicknamed them "The Peach Fuzz Gang" because everyone was only 19 years old and hadn't even started shaving yet. Davey's racing schedule was packed, as the "Peach Fuzz Gang" traveled to tracks all over the Southeast.

As a young driver, Davey had a lot to learn. At almost every race, he would skid along the fence or veer off into the grandstand, and his car suffered all kinds of wear and tear. But he'd go home and work night and day to put the car back together. A week later, he'd be ready for another race.

From his first race, April 22, 1979, in Birmingham, Alabama, Davey made a big impression. Driving a 1972 Chevy Nova he'd borrowed from his Uncle Donnie, he came in fifth place—an astonishing finish given his youth and lack of experience. Five races later, he would amaze even more people by coming in first place.

In the early 1980s, Davey had a string of triumphs racing in a series run by the Automobile Racing Club of America (ARCA). These ARCA races were a good testing ground for Davey. Here, through trial and error, he sharpened his talents and gained experience. He began to win more and more races until, in 1985, he was named ARCA's all-time leader in superspeedway wins.

In the next few years, Davey got several tastes of Winston Cup racing. In 1985, he made his debut at the Talladega, Alabama, track—close to his home of Hueytown. Davey finished tenth, a truly impressive outing for someone of his age and experience.

In 1986, a lucky break got him another chance to drive in a Winston Cup race and earned him even more attention. Car owner Junior Johnston asked Davey to take over for his driver, Neil Bonnett, in a race. During the race, Davey pulled into the lead; after he was passed, he was able to regain the lead. Although he only finished in seventh place, his performance was particularly noticed in the racing world.

At around the time Davey was making himself known in his first few professional wins, several car owners—Harry Rainier, Jay T. Lundi, and Robert Yates—were looking for a new driver. Even though Davey had much less experience than other drivers, they were impressed by his determination and willingness to take risks.

Davey Allison loses a tire at the 1987 Daytona 500. He made it to the pits and rejoined the race.

They decided to take their own risk, and hired Davey as their driver.

In 1987, Davey stormed onto the NASCAR scene at the Daytona 500. Racing at exceptionally high speeds in the qualifying runs, he not only qualified to participate in the race but earned a first row spot—quite a debut for a rookie. His owners, who joked of betting against Davey, were pleasantly surprised by his performance.

After this sudden success at the start of the season, Davey soon got a reminder just how dangerous racing in the professionals could be. It happened at the superspeedway in Darlington, South Carolina, known as one of the most perilous tracks in the circuit. Davey and another car smashed into one another, and Davey skidded off the course, spinning rapidly as he plowed through some wooden poles. There was a BANG! as the car burst into flames.

Fortunately, Davey wasn't seriously injured by the explosion. But he knew now that he was racing with the big boys. The car he had crashed into was none other than that of the great Bobby Allison.

A month later, Davey once again found himself on the same track as his father, at what they had come to think of as their "home track" at Talladega. This time, though, it was Bobby who became involved in a death-defying crash. About 21 laps into the race, Bobby's car became airborne. It flipped over and crashed heavily to the earth.

Looking in his rearview mirror at the wreckage, Davey feared the worst; he couldn't imagine his father had survived that crash. He was also concerned because he thought there was no way other cars could avoid hitting his father.

For what seemed like an eternity, Davey circled the track until he was in a position to see his father. As he came around the turn, he saw his father waving at him. He was OK!

Feeling intense relief, Davey sailed on to win the race, earning himself a spot on "victory lane." That race made Davey the first rookie to win a Winston Cup race since 1981. A few weeks later, another win at Dover, Delaware, helped earn him the title of rookie of the year. Clearly, there was a new Allison making headlines.

The start of the 1988 racing season, Davey's second year of Winston Cup racing, began with his famous second-place finish against his father. Before the race, Davey said he planned to use some of the same tricks he'd learned from his father against his father. What he wound up learning, though, was that his father hadn't taught him all the tricks he knew.

In his first few years on the Winston Cup circuit, Davey had earned several wins. Owing to his many victories, as well as his charm, energy and youthful enthusiasm, he had also won over a healthy following of fans. More and more crowds of people came to watch Davey race.

In the racing world, though, he gained a reputation for being somewhat of a wild card. He drove very fast, but did not always use his head. As a result, he sometimes made bad decisions that got him into trouble. He took these losses very hard and became extremely frustrated with himself.

In the middle of the 1991 season, Larry McReynolds became his crew chief and the leader of his team. McReynolds had watched Davey win his first race back in 1979. Throughout the years, he followed Davey's career and had a real understanding of Davey's individual talents. McReynolds knew that Davey's greatest strength was his aggressiveness; it was also his biggest weakness.

Davey, like his father, was a tough driver, willing to take all kinds of risks. Sometimes, though, his aggression prevented him from thinking clearly. He would wind up right in the middle of a major smashup or skirmish that he could have easily avoided. Encouraging Davey to assess situations on the track more carefully, McReynolds taught Davey how to make his aggressive tendencies work for him. McReynolds showed Davey that by holding back at times, his chances of winning were much greater.

Additionally, the new team, led by McReynolds, worked very well together. The members of the crew listened to one another's views and respected each other. With this new team, Davey won

Davey sits in his car as it is checked after a practice run.

11 of his 19 career victories. Unlike his father, Davey was fortunate to find a team he liked so much early on in his career. Like all good racers, Davey always acknowledged that a great deal of his success came from having such strong support behind him.

Just how much Davey had matured as a driver became clear to everyone at the start of the 1992 season at the Daytona 500. That race is remembered as the site of one the largest crashes in Daytona history—a 14-car pileup that foiled the hopes of victory of nearly half the drivers. The accident occurred when Sterling Marlin tried to pass the car in front of him, driven by Bill Elliott. As Marlin pulled out from behind Elliott, Ernie Irvan got directly behind Marlin in order

Davey Allison takes the checkered flag at the 1992 Daytona 500 ahead of Morgan Shepard.

to take advantage of the draft and to try to pass Elliott.

Marlin pushed the car's accelerator, but the car just could not gain enough speed to complete the pass. Meanwhile, Irvan had built up speed and decided to try to pass Elliot himself.

As a result, the three cars (Elliott's, Marlin's, and Irvan's) were lined up, one alongside the other, as they came around the turn into the backstretch. Here, the track narrows down to two lanes, and there was no way all three cars could possibly fit.

Marlin realized what was happening and tried to slow down, but there wasn't enough time. As the track narrowed, he was sandwiched between the two other cars. The cars bumped one another and all three began to spin out of control, forming a treacherous whirlpool for the other cars coming around the turn. As cars came speeding out of the turn, the drivers had no choice but to head directly into the mass of cars.

Davey, however, was not one of them. He had been right behind Ernie Irvan and could have stayed there. However, he had learned that cars can't make those fast turns at Daytona three abreast without some serious trouble. He thought to himself, "this is not for me," and held back. As a result, he avoided being caught up in the major pileup.

Davey later admitted to the press that a year earlier he would have probably been right at the center of the pile. "But I've grown up a lot, especially in the last 12 months," he told the *New York Times.*

Throughout the race, Davey demonstrated this kind of smart yet tough driving. He managed to hold the lead for a remarkable 127 laps of the 200-lap race.

Davey drove on to take the Daytona, earning his place in victory lane as his father had done three times before. Davey and Bobby were only the second father and son duo to have won at Daytona.

Unlike many other professional sports, race car driving is extremely dangerous. It may be incredibly exciting, but the fact is that each time a driver gets behind the wheel of the car, he puts his life at risk.

When cars are going at such high speeds, they become very difficult to control. When you get so many cars on the same track driving at those speeds, there's bound to be trouble.

Good drivers can take action to lessen the impact of a crash. When the car is spinning, for example, they can try to maneuver the car away from the others in the race and avoid causing a major pileup. However, mishaps on the track

Davey Allison climbs out of his car as relief driver Bobby Hillin (center) takes his place during the running of the Taladega 500. Allison, then second in the Winston Cup points standing, started the race despite having been injured in a crash the week before and having left the hospital only three days earlier.

often happen without warning. In these cases, the driver can only hope for the best.

The sturdy race cars are built to take a great deal of wear and tear. The body of the car, although completely smashed, can protect the driver and leave him unharmed. If there is a major impact, though, the driver can become badly injured.

Professional race car drivers understand the extreme dangers involved in their chosen sport. They make certain to take whatever precautions they can and try to drive as safely as possible on the track. They watch out for their own safety as well as for the other drivers. They also realize, though, that many factors are out of their control and that their life is always at risk.

Several times, the Allisons were forced to face tragedy on the track. Each time, their love for one another as well as their courage helped them get through these difficult periods. The admirable way they pulled through these tragedies earned them immense respect in the racing world. The Allisons are a symbol of the kind of bravery and dedication it takes to succeed in the sport.

In 1981, Donnie was involved in a major crash in a race at Charlotte. While Donnie had been involved in many minor crashes during his career, this was a much more serious one. In addition to bumps and bruises, Donnie suffered major injuries to the head. He tried to continue racing but found it too difficult. A few weeks later, he decided to retire from racing for good.

After Bobby's fantastic 1988 Daytona victory, a similarly devastating crash would change his life and put an abrupt end to his successful career. At the Pocono, Pennsylvania, raceway, Bobby was looking for his second championship win of the season. In the first lap, only seconds into the race, he was involved in a multiple car crash. Several cars, traveling at speeds of 170 mph, knocked into his Buick, sending him smashing into the fence. It was the kind of crash that no one believed he could possibly survive. Bobby had to be cut out of the mangled car. Critically injured, with major injuries all over his body, Bobby hovered close to death. Suffering from severe brain damage, he remained in a coma for several weeks.

Davey was suddenly called upon to take his father's place as head of the family. The night of his father's accident, he helped his mother make the difficult decision to give permission for his father to have the risky brain surgery that was his only hope for a recovery.

To the surprise of many, Bobby did recover, but it took a long time during which Bobby was in intense pain. Even after he was released from the hospital, he was never quite the same. The accident seriously affected his memory and sense of balance. As a result, he was forced to retire from racing.

Davey took the accident very hard. "It really didn't change my attitude about racing but it had a tremendous effect on me personally," he said.

With his father in the hospital, Davey also found himself in the position of acting as the head of the family. In addition to caring for his father, he had to manage the responsibilities of the entire Allison family. He had to get used to the extra responsibility of having family members come to him for advice and support.

Davey also had personal responsibilities. After getting married in 1989, he and his wife, Liz, started a family. Not long after Bobby's accident, they had a girl, Krista. A year later, they had a son, Robert.

Davey eventually had the satisfaction of watching his father become involved in racing again, in a different capacity. In 1990, Bobby became a stock-car owner. Mike Alexander served as the team's driver. At that year's Daytona, Davey noticed how his father, so happy to be at the racetrack again, seemed to glow. Bobby's fellow racers were also glad to see him. Many stopped by to say hello and to ask Bobby for some last minute tips.

In July, Davey raced at Pocono, the very same track where his father had been in that devastating crash. As Davey was making his way through a pack of cars, he collided with another car. Skidding to the center of the track, Davey's car flipped over and over. In all, his car flipped 11 times before it could stop. As the car turned, parts flew all over the track, until only a skeleton-like shell remained. Davey was tossed and turned inside, without the protection of the car's body and outer frame.

Bobby Allison gives the thumbs up after recuperating from life-threatening surgery.

Miraculously, Davey had survived, but he was badly injured. He spent the next several days in the hospital, with a broken arm and collarbone, broken ribs, and a concussion. Bruised from head to toe, he lay in the hospital in intense pain.

Even a bad experience like this accident taught Davey valuable lessons. Davey later remarked that everyone has a tendency to take things for granted, to feel they're "bullet proof" until they get a harsh reminder that they're still human. He said, "an accident like at Pocono brings you back down to earth and makes you realize we're all human and we're all very vulnerable."

The accident changed Davey's outlook on his life. In the hospital, he started to think about what was really important to him. He realized how much he loved and valued his family. After he recovered, he began to spend much more time with his wife and children.

Only six days after this major accident, Davey got right back in his race car. After having been in such a major accident and in such pain, he found it terrifying to get back inside the car. But he knew how important it was for him to overcome his fear if he hoped to continue racing. His crew had to tape his hands to the steering wheel so that he could control the vehicle. Before turning the car over to another driver, he managed to complete five laps. To his crew, fellow racers and fans, this was a sign of Davey's courage as well as his dedication to the sport.

That 1992 season that had so much glory for Davey, especially at the Daytona 500, was also to have one of the saddest tragedies in the Allison family. Davey and his brother, Clifford, like any brothers, were very close, but also very different. They had their fights and their competitions, as brothers always do. But they also shared the same love for racing.

At 27 years old, Clifford was also forging his own racing career in the Bush Grand National series. In the few races in which he drove, he showed great promise. Clifford had the same instinctive flair for aggressive driving as his father and brother. But in August 1992, his career was sadly cut short. While practicing for a qualifying run in Brooklyn, Michigan, Clifford's car spun out of control. He was killed in the crash.

Davey was shocked by his brother's accident. "Clifford's death hit close to home and it hit awful hard" he said. But Davey did gain comfort knowing that Clifford was doing what he loved. "That part of it makes me happy," he said, "I know he might have died but he died happy."

After Clifford's accident, Davey took comfort the best way he knew how. He went ahead with his plan to race that weekend. Many people criticized him for going ahead with a race just after his brother had died, but Davey believed it was what his brother would have wanted. It was also the best way he knew of to deal with his own grief.

Davey managed to finish fifth in that race at Michigan, in what was probably the most emotionally difficult race of his career. It demonstrated to the entire racing world the Allison family's devotion to the sport that meant so much to them all.

Davey kept on driving one race at a time, grappling with various setbacks while maintaining an impressive overall standing in the Winston Cup circuit. Several weeks after his brother's death, at a race in Georgia, he needed to finish in sixth place or better to earn enough points to make him Winston Cup champion. With less than 100 laps to go, Davey was running precisely in sixth place. An unfortunate action caused by another driver, Ernie Irvan, forced him out of the race and shattered his chance at a championship win.

Davey reacted with disappointment but also an acceptance of the loss that showed how much he had matured as a driver. Early in his career, Davey would take these losses very hard and often become quite angry. But he had now been racing long enough to understand that life in the fast lane has its thrills, but its costs as well. He had learned that when you hit a bump in the road, you have to just keep on going.

After that loss, Davey told the press, "We didn't get it so we'll just go back and we'll get ready for next year and come out and try again."

Davey came into the 1993 season with his typical optimism and self-confidence. But on July 12, while attempting to land a helicopter he was flying in a parking lot at Talladega—his beloved "home" track where he had earned so many of his victories—something went wrong. The helicopter crashed. Davey died several hours later from massive head injuries he had sustained in the crash.

Davey was only 32 when he died, and everyone agreed he would have certainly gone on to greater glory on the track. Yet his career was filled with great success. He had 19 Winston Cup wins, including that 1992 Daytona 500. His total winnings, $6.7 million, put him 10th on the all-time career list. The Sunday before the accident, he had finished third in a race in London, New Hampshire, placing him fifth in the 1993 Winston Cup standing.

Davey was mourned by thousands of people. His warmth and charisma had won him an incredible following of fans as well as the respect and love of his fellow racers and their families. At his funeral, 600 racing people attended, while an estimated 4,000 fans watched from a distance.

Indianapolis racing champion Mario Andretti probably best phrased the racing world's reaction to the tragedies the Allisons had suffered. When questioned by the *New York Times*, Andretti said, "Why? It is beyond my compre-

Liz Allison, holding Krista, during prerace ceremonies at the Taladega Superspeedway. Officials dedicated the race to Davey Allison, who had died in a helicopter crash at the racetrack.

hension. If ever there was goodness in anyone, it is in that family. The whole family. They are the example of goodness."

Davey himself, however, understood that life is filled with these kinds of risks—on or off the race course. That's why throughout his life he emphasized the importance of trying to do what you love and trying to do your best. Davey had spent his life doing something that he truly loved. You can't ask for a greater gift than that.

STATISTICS

Year	Winner	Average Speed

DAYTONA 500

Year	Winner	Average Speed
1978	Bobby Allison	159.730
1982	Bobby Allison	153.991
1988	Bobby Allison	137.531
1992	Davey Allison	160.256

SOUTHERN 500

Year	Winner	Average Speed
1971	Bobby Allison	131.398
1972	Bobby Allison	128.124
1975	Bobby Allison	116.825
1983	Bobby Allison	123.343

TALLADEGA 500

Year	Winner	Average Speed
1971	Donnie Allison	145.945
1977	Donnie Allison	162.524

WORLD 600

Year	Winner	Average Speed
1970	Donnie Allison	129.680
1971	Bobby Allison	140.442
1981	Bobby Allison	129.326
1984	Bobby Allison	129.233
1991	Davey Allison	138.951

Note: These four races can be considered the backbone of the NASCAR tour. The Daytona 500 is the richest race, the Southern 500 is the oldest, the Talladega 500 the fastest, and the World 600 is the longest.

AN ALLISON FAMILY CHRONOLOGY

1959   Bobby and Donnie leave Miami in search of greater racing opportunities; they eventually settle in Hueytown, Alabama.

1965   After years of success in the modified circuit, Bobby decides to move up to the NASCAR Winston Cup Grand Nationals.

1966   Donnie follows in Bobby's footsteps, moving up to the Grand Nationals.

1971   In one of the most famous finishes in NASCAR history, Donnie edges out Bobby for a win at the Winston 500. Overall, though, 1971 is Bobby's year, as he takes seven superspeedway victories.

1978   After a major career slump that lasted three seasons in which he would not win in 67 races, Bobby makes a major comeback by taking the Daytona 500.

1979   Davey Allison drives in his first major race with an impressive fifth place finish at Birmingham.

1981   Donnie is forced to retire after sustaining massive head injuries in a crash at Charlotte.

1982   Bobby wins the Daytona a second time, becoming only the third driver to win it more than once.

1983   After over 20 years of racing and after losing by only a handful of points in '81 and '82, Bobbie becomes Winston Cup champion.

1987   Davey storms onto the NASCAR scene by qualifying for a first row spot at the Daytona and is named rookie of the year.

1988   Bobby takes the Daytona a third time, with Davey a close second. Bobby is the oldest man to ever win a Winston Cup race. A few weeks later, major injuries sustained in a devastating crash at Pocono raceway forces Bobby to retire.

1991   Davey follows in his father's footsteps, winning the Daytona 500.

1992   Clifford is killed after crashing his car in a practice run in Michigan.

1993   Davey dies after receiving major head injuries in a helicopter crash. Thousands of fans and members of the racing world mourn his loss.

2000   *Full Circle: The Story of Davey Allison*, written by Davey's widow, Liz, is released.

SUGGESTIONS FOR FURTHER READING AND VIEWING

Books

Auto Racing by Charles Coombs (New York: William Morrow, 1971).

Behind the Wall: A Season on the NASCAR Circuit by Richard Huff (Chicago: Bonus Books, 1992).

Drama on the Speedway by Ross R. Olney (New York: William Morrow, 1978).

The Encyclopedia of Auto Racing Greats by Robert Cutter and Bob Fendell (Englewood Cliffs: Prentice Hall, 1973).

King Richard by Bill Libby (New York: Doubleday, 1977).

Modern Auto Racing Superstars by Ross R. Olney (New York: Dodd, Mead and Company, 1978).

Racin' the NASCAR Winston Cup Stock Car Racing Series by George Gilliam and Mark Meyer (Charlottesville, VA: Howell Press, 1989).

Winston Cup Racing by Sallie Stephenson (New York: Macmillan Children's Group, 1991).

Videos

The Davey Allison Story: Reflections of Davey (produced by Cabin Fever Entertainment, Inc., 1994).

Daytona: Drama, Danger, Dedication (produced by CBS Sports, 1991).

A Crash Course in Racing. (produced by Cabin Fever Entertainment, Inc., 1989).

A Week in the Life of a Race Team (produced by DSL Communications, Inc., 1992).

ABOUT THE AUTHOR

A professional writer, Steven Frank is the author of *Magic Johnson* (Chelsea House), *A+ Term Papers*, and *Sample Business Letters and Memos* (both for Longmeadow Press), as well as numerous articles. He currently teaches at New York University, where he received his M.A. He lives in New York City.

INDEX

Alexander, Mike, 56
Allison, Bobby
  injuries of, 11, 19, 20, 34, 47, 54–55
  victories of, 9–15, 19, 27, 31, 34, 37, 41
Allison, Bonnie, 21
Allison, Carrie, 21
Allison, Clifford, 21, 43, 57–58
Allison, Davey
  injuries of, 56, 59
  victories of, 45, 47, 48, 51, 59
Allison, Donald, 21
Allison, Donnie
  injuries of, 20, 54
  victories of, 30, 31
Allison, E. J., 9–10, 17, 18, 44
Allison, Eddie, 26
Allison, Kenney, 21
Allison, Kittie, 9–10, 18
Allison, Krista, 56, 60
Allison, Liz, 55–56, 60
Allison, Pam, 21
Allison, Robert, 56
Allison, Ronald, 21
Allison, Tommy, 19
Andretti, Mario, 59–60
Baker, Buddy, 13–14, 30, 31, 36
Bodine, Brett, 12
Bonnett, Neil, 35, 45
Boy Scouts, 28
Daytona 500, 9–15, 29, 35–37, 38, 46,
  49–51, 56, 57

DiGard/Gatorade team, 37
Elliott, Bill, 50–51
Firecracker 400, 28, 30
Foyt, A. J., 36
Guthrie, Janet, 33
Hillin, Bobby, 53
Hutcherson, Ron, 36
Irvan, Ernie, 50–51, 58
Johnston, Junior, 45
Lilly, Betty, 26
Lundi, Jay T., 45
Marcis, Dave, 31
Marlin, Sterling, 50–51
McReynolds, Larry, 48
Moore, Bud, 35
Nelson, Gary, 37
Parsons, Benny, 36
Peach Fuzz Gang, 44
Petty, Richard, 12, 29–30, 41
Pond, Lenny, 36
Prickett, Clyde, 26
Rainier, Harry, 45
Sunderman, Robert, 19
Turner, Curtis, 27
Waltrip, Darrell, 39–40
World 600, 41
Yarborough, Cale, 36, 37, 38, 39, 41
Yates, Robert, 45
